"When beautiful poetry emerges from its secret abode, we can only hope we have been wise enough to leave our soul's door ajar, and that it will enter and find a home there.

I have read Leonard A. Slade, Jr.'s poetry, and I am the better for it, the wiser for it, and the happier for it."

— Dr. Maya Angelou
Reynolds Professor of American Studies
Wake Forest University

"Leonard A. Slade, Jr., is a traditionalist. However, you will find in his work the twists and wry music and risks of the contemporary.

The mixture is appealing."

—Gwendoyn Brooks
Pulitzer Prize Winner
Poet Laureate of Illinois

"*Pure Light* is going to be a winner, with its many fine poems, its musical qualities, its exuberance, and the close observations, often wryly stated."

—Professor George Hendrick
Department of English
The University of Illinois

"In *Pure Light*, Leonard Slade meditates on the most intimate of relationships, those with family, friends, and, yes, even the intimate relationships we have with our heroes. He parts the curtain on that intimacy and, in language that whispers intensely, reveals the fine delicate tremors of pure, raw passion."

—Professor Yvonne Jackson
ɔartment of English
bash College

PURE LIGHT

BOOK OF POEMS

BY

LEONARD A. SLADE, JR.

PURE LIGHT

BOOK OF POEMS

BY

LEONARD A. SLADE, JR.

The McGraw-Hill Companies, Inc.

New York   St. Louis   San Francisco   Auckland   Bogotá
Caracas   Lisbon   London   Madrid   Mexico   Milan   Montreal
New Delhi   Paris   San Juan   Singapore   Sydney   Tokyo   Toronto

McGraw-Hill

*A Division of The **McGraw·Hill** Companies*

ISBN: 0-07-057963-6
Library of Congress Catalog Card Number 96-77747

Editor: M. A. Hollander
Cover Design: Maggie Lytle
Interior Design: Lydia Zabarsky & Reuben Kantor
Printer/Binder: Bookmart Press

For my wife

Roberta Hall

For my daughter

Minitria Elisabeth

AKNOWLEDGMENTS

I am grateful to several readers who have suggested ways to improve this volume, *Pure Light*. I am especially indebted to Eugene Garber (Ph.D., University of Iowa), of the State University of New York at Albany; George Hendrick (Ph.D., University of Texas), of the University of Illinois; Yvonne Jackson (B.A., Yale, and M.F.A., University of Alabama), of Wabash College; Roberta Hall-Slade (M.M., University of Chicago), of Siena College; Minitria Elisabeth Slade (student, University of Michigan at Ann Arbor), and Debbie Bourassa, of the State University of New York at Albany. The ardent support of these two persons is no less appreciated: Allen Ballard (Ph.D., Harvard University), of the State University of New York at Albany; and Karen Hitchcock (Ph.D., University of Rochester), also of the State University of New York at Albany.

CONTENTS

POETRY

Poetry Continued

About the Author

"When I consider how
my light is spent,
Ere half my days, in this dark world...
my soul more bent
To serve my Maker, and present
My true account...
'They also serve who only stand and wait.'"
—JOHN MILTON
"When I consider how my light is spent"

PURE LIGHT

In the evening were the glowing
moon and shining stars, a gift
moving the world. Brighter
now, rays of light,
glimmer of hope; unborn child
on a donkey sleeping in darkness.
We were falling in
Eden, Virgin Mother.
We were waiting on edge
for a new world, for centuries:
praying for you to give birth to
new love and pure light.

NEW YORK

The Northeast is a Mecca
Creating cultures for Sweetness and Light.
Richer now,
Wall Street
World Trade
United Nations
Schomberg
NBC
Carnegie Hall.
Old and new,
Black and white,
Precious and priceless,
I celebrate
New love.

THE HARLEM BOYS' CHOIR

Sounds
of pureness
send love through the

air. The Black Boys
hum beauty and
stand majestic

Touching spectators'
hearts
light now—echoes

of the past
produce sorrow,
and melodies

of the present
celebrate a future
belonging to them.

ONE MILLION BLACK MEN'S MARCH

In this powerful city Washington, D.C.,
I see Black men holding hands,
And purple gums hollering for freedom
And Black leaders singing songs
Dreaming of brotherhood.

All the proud fathers celebrate solidarity,
Their women stay home to watch,
Honoring their heroes.

Reborn
These Black men grow more beautiful
At the end of day
And return home cutting darkness
Hoping for love.

1996

(ALLING ALL BLACK MEN

Calling all Black men
Real
Responsible
Rich in love.

All Black men
Eligible
for
Black women

To love
and
Hold
Forever.

Calling all Black men
Come on
Home Now!

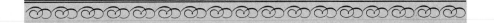

JULY

Americans are cheering and celebrating with balloons and fireworks,
        Stars rising and falling cutting darkness.
Three booms move the Earth,
        Orange moon bleeding the sky.

GROWING WITH GRACE

You joined me in the Green Mountains
of Bennington, Vermont,
resting in a cottage by the road. I

flirted with your eyes, entered
your mind and body to celebrate
the ups and down of the years. I

was more than your lover that night
when you whispered gentle words
and sipped champagne. I

was your friend, discovering
sweet ways to love the new years,
growing older with grace.

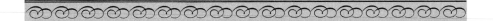

"Who knoweth the spirit of man
that goeth upward, and
the spirit of the beast that
goeth downward to the earth?"
—ECCLESIASTES
Chapter 3, Verse 21

THE UNABOMBER

The Unabomber brilliantly multiplies and subtracts,
yet scribbles missives with problems defined—

so rustic out in the country,
now it's time for a crucifixion.

Letters have blown the world to pieces,
everything stands still in time.

Neither prison nor gas can destroy
the pain and sorrow immersed in tears.

10 April 1996

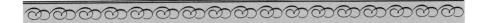

INDOMITABLE SPIRIT

It's an indomitable spirit
you give us, mean racists:

Burn Black churches in the South
and choke on your own hate.

We're here to stay.

FIRE LIGHTING THE WORLD

According to USA Today
when blacks slept
it was quiet

until a white man roamed
Southern black churches
planting something

secretly
near
the center of the altar

where Jesus' cross
hanging in darkness
waited for light.

Later
an explosion reduced
a structure to splinters

and
fire
lit the world.

DEAR SUSAN SMITH

I am trying to forgive you
with my broken heart.

I wake at 3 a.m. praying for you.
The images of your two sons haunt me,
and I can barely breathe.

If your sons rise from the grave
together, maybe

surprise the world with smiles
and waves.
I still dream, a

prisoner of eternal sorrow.

2 August 1995

IN PRAISE OF SHOESHINES

We suffered shining shoes for 300 years.
Then, one day, this bootery up North had a bargain:

>   buy your shoes,
>   get free shoeshines for life.

Chocolate brother bought beautiful brown shoes
from a cold vanilla sister on Saturday.

Now, he returns often for shoeshines on Sunday
and the sister rolls her bad blue eyes

forgetting history.

SET THE RECORD STRAIGHT

Change the history books for all
Present truth
Beginning with Africa
Landing in the Americas

Killing lies whatever recorded—
Nkrumah and Nat Turner
John Brown and Abe Lincoln
Martin Luther King and Malcolm X

Write it down
Write it down.
Write it down.

THE PRIZE

We are not born to have glory
for work done from sunrise to sunset:
it is not wise to seek gold
showered from earthly kingdoms.

Yet we die before the gods
carve our works in stone.

TENURE

Tenure is a cherished concept
promising eternal happiness in the
world of work. Sometimes, it's grinning
and butt-kissing, teaching and serving
publishing and creating and making love
to the moon.

WORDS

Be careful what you say.
When you use words, it
  is hard to take them back,
They pierce heavy hearts, aching hearts; they
  kill friends quickly; they don't care—
Be careful what you say.

15 March 1996

I FLY AWAY

Sometimes
after church service,
I talk to white folk
My black suit is so dapper.
My wide straw hat
fights the hot sun
while I sip lemonade
and laugh
with blacks and whites
savoring social intercourse
under a Maple tree.
I am cool, cool, so cool.
Then Miss Manners points
to my "fly" in public,
asking,
"What's that you've got there?"
Half my shirt rests outside my pants.
I quickly pull my shirt
inside the proper place.
Laughter from the crowd
accompanies my embarrassment.
Miss Manners is secure now,
having bruised an ego,
evoked laughter, and
tasted power.
She turns red with her smile
and walks away
with her other half.
I strut in the opposite direction,
black and beautiful and proud
of what she did not know.

THIS WAS A MAN

This man was the first Black American
to earn a doctorate from Harvard University,
an intellectual giant who interpreted Black

culture; he was born in the North, taught in
the South—enlightening the poor, instructing
the destitute. He studied the meaning of progress

and gave us books and journals and the NAACP; he wrote
sorrow songs of the oppressed, lifted the burdens
of the downtrodden. He inspired talented Blacks

(lawyers and doctors, preachers and teachers,
business professionals and community leaders),
changing a human race. Education was his

weapon for the struggle of equality, for the
taste of justice. He proved Blacks proud
and beautiful, regal and strong. Our

souls are rooted in his whole being, bitter and sweet,
hard and long suffering. He dreamed of
freedom. This was a man, W.E.B.

DR. DUBOIS

Dr. DuBois! you should be breathing now;
America needs you: some are children
Of crack and cocaine, AIDS, murders,
Crimes, street gangs, prostitution, and prisons.
Have changed our culture forever
Of eternal happiness. America suffers;
Speak to us, return, please!
Your *Souls of Black Folk* was our hope.
Your voice was prophetic,
Changing like the seasons, predicting
Spring and winter between races,
Yet you sleep while we work another century.

BUDGET CUTS

On the streets, in
hospitals
destitute
they're there—poor
as beggars, ashamed
as misers but visible
more and more—
asking the politicians
Why?
You can see their eyes
absorbing pain now
closing
and morticians
bringing caskets
for rest.

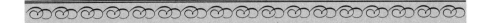

TODAY WE ARE RISING

Machines replace Black fingers
in the fields,
a people now doing their thing—
We are everywhere and everything:
a governor, senators, lawyers, doctors,
professors, writers, artists, everything
freedom wants us to be. Today we are
rising, rising, rising in love
and desire to make the world new.

THE CRUISE

Such a smooth sailing
through the breeze of summer and into

the Atlantic, carrying thousands on the
deck! Buffets and music

create our strength and our hearts
cry for rest but we

enjoy, banging it up. There's nothing
more pleasurable than social intercourse.

Screaming is for couples celebrating
love, and bodies move

for hours hungry for more.
Gambling is nothing

when happiness is born,
The Ecstasy moves on,

couples knocking it up
with song and desire

they climb into bed and penetrate the night,
making love complete.

YOUR LIFE IS OVER FOR YOU IF

you smoke ten packs of cigarettes daily
guzzle Jack Daniel to sleep as ritual
sit at your oak desk fifteen hours daily
take (always) the elevator instead of walking (briskly)
marry a fussbudget who worships materialism
have children that you do not want
eat fat hogs and quarts of ice cream to break fast
destroy bridges instead of building them in relationships
hate instead of loving with all your heart.

"Where are the songs of Spring?"
—JOHN KEATS
"To Autumn"

SUNRISE

How orange the sky is this morning
with sunlight breaking cotton clouds.

Fog by the river is ghostlike
and so is the hoo of the owl.

Birds sing in tall birches,
cocks crow in the barnyard.

Gum eyes open slowly—one peek
and a new day is born.

WHY I WILL NOT BE A CHILD AGAIN

My demons hide
like ghosts after dark:
there is no fear
of light. I will curse
like them the rest
of my life, even
beyond the grave.
Childhood memories make
a hell for adult goodness.
I am lonely in church.
I am eccentric at home.

It is winter.
I feel cold.
I see my child
sleighriding,
cutting acres of snow.
I am the river.
I am the mountain.
I am the forest.

My soul catches fire—
I am the sun.
I am the moon.
I am a morning star.

SUMMER

Summer, among days of warmth,
bodies tan on beaches —
calypso music dancing us.
Swim suits flirt their parts
and eyeballs roll and roll.
I, too, become drunk with beauty
eager for love.

PLUMS

Gradually the leaves turned green,
Spring,
Which had buried winter for birth,
Grew sunny and breezy,
Suddenly
From some small blossoming tree
Hundreds of petals pink and pretty
Brightened the field,
Waiting for sweet
Plums to come.

15 March 1996

MOLLY

She struts the fields sunrise to sunset
Pulling the plow that cuts black soil. I
Hold the handles as sweat falls,
And pull her ropes right and left.
She huffs and puffs and pulls.
Five years old, I run and follow
Now stop to rub her nose and ears,
Her breadth bad and hot with foam.
I lead her to water where
She thinks and drinks
To fill her belly to relieve the pain.
Molly my friend my pet my all
Proudly plows deep and long
Then leans to Mother Earth
To taste delicious worms.

"God is love...."

—1 CORINTHIANS

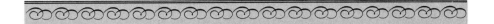

GOD

Is the light in my dark
In my corner
Where demons are fools
In my closet

I know Satan's ways
He's crazy
To be sneaky and
To make war with love.

WORSHIP

An army of choir members
entering one door

of a small country church
marched in singing

"We're marching to Zion
We're marching to Zion"

rocking their brown bodies
raising their right hands and

lifting their melodious voices
singing and marching.

Outside a choir of birds
came to attention and listened.

SO HAPPY

Sister Rosetta rejoices.
—but we glide back
in our church seats.
What hair.
What a voice.

That's just Sister Rosetta
jumping toward Heaven
every Sunday, stomping
her feet
waving her hands

calling His name
clinching her fists
hollering and singing
about her love
for Jesus.

(Her wig landing in my lap.)

It's all right.
It's all right
It's all right.

INNOCENCE IN BLACK AND WHITE

Sitting alone in my row at the Cathedral,
I kneel for prayer.
After the sermon and preparation for communion,
I begin my slow walk to the altar.
A five-year-old white child then glides
down the aisle to join me.
I smile and let her cross my path
to kneel with me.
Dropping her *Book of Common Prayer*, she smiles
at me over her perceived faux pas.
Assisting her with the right page
of another Book, I read with her
the same words, symbols with meanings
that transcend the now and contradict history.
She follows me to the altar to kneel
for the same blood
indifferent to my Blackness.
After partaking of the Supper,
she follows me to my seat
satisfied that a communion of two bodies
has elevated two souls
for all the world to see.

ARM AROUND A SON
AT A NORTH CAROLINA AIRPORT

I love to see you viewing tv basketball
Hugging your Black son
Watching together the NCAA Tournament
Saying nothing
But being one
In Black love.

ONE MORE TIME

They are weepers in church,
gliding the aisle with hugs
and in dark suits holding on:

family and friends—a hunchback daddy and
a grayheaded son console a twelve-year-old
daughter in this place of mourners,

where a black preacher and thirteen
choir members sing "Nearer My God to Thee"
accompanying the Organ's sad sounds,

still crying and calling "O God" but
reaching the casket one more time
before saying goodbye to Mom.

TO RONALD HARMON BROWN

I heard from newsmen you may be flying
   over a mountain near Bosnia.

Gusty winds send torrents of rain
   and now I worry in the dark on my knees.

Bolts of lightning strike a big bird
   but my dream tonight will be pleasant.

When morning comes, I wake to learn
   a nightmare of you burned and broken
   my heart heavy.

HE'S MY BROTHER
(FOR MAURICE)

All night
  I daydream
    in the hard bed
      while stars fall,

burning
  glorious thoughts
    of my brother's
      precious past.

    Once
I saw him celebrate people
  touching the heart's core
  and
      it was wonderful.

I don't want to think anymore
  about all the things
    I could have told him
      that flesh will become dust or ashes, morning

will force me to
  reconsider
    being and nothingness
      my sense and place

in the universe
  and after that brood awhile
    but cherish him
      and his unconditional love.

I want to disappear
  in the sky,
    become the stars
      I want to suffer myself

on brother's bed
  accepting
    believing
      his departure is mine.

HOW GREAT YOU ARE

You made the cradle of the earth.
You made clouds for the Heavens.
You made the high hills
and the low valleys.
You assigned the moon for the seasons.
You gave knowledge to the sun.
You made darkness into light.
You laid the foundation of the world.
You gave us Africa and Asia,
North America and South America.
You shared the entire universe.
You caused grass to grow.
You brought food out of the earth.
You traveled the mighty oceans.
You stilled the raging seas.
You dwell in all generations.
You are clothed with honor
and wrapped with majesty and rich in love.
You are our everlasting God.

30 June 1995
Nassau, Bahamas

ABOUT THE AUTHOR

LEONARD A. SLADE, JR., grew up on North Carolina. He is the author of *Another Black Voice: A Different Drummer* (1988), *The Beauty of Blackness* (1989), *I Fly Like a Bird* (1992), *The Whipping Song* (1993), *Vintage* (1995), *Fire Burning* (1995), and editor of *Black Essays* (1995). Among many of his awards, he has been the recipient of The Kentucky Humanities Council Grant, The Southern Conference on Afro-American Studies Award, The U.S. Department of State Fellowship for Postdoctoral Study in West Africa, The Hudson-Mohawk Association of Colleges and Universities Award, The Northeast Modern Language Association Research Grant, the Ford Foundation Fellowship, and two Excellence in Teaching Awards. He teaches at the State University of New York at Albany, and lives in Albany with his wife and daughter. *Pure Light* is his seventh collection of poems.